DATE DUE

The Titanic
1912

The Loss of an Unsinkable Liner

VIC PARKER

CHICAGO, ILLINOIS

© 2006 Raintree
a division of Reed Elsevier Inc.
Chicago, Illinois

Customer Service 888-363-4266
Visit our website at www.heinemannraintree.com

Designed by Victoria Bevan and AMR Design Ltd
Illustrations by David Woodroffe
Printed and bound in China by South China Printing
  Company

10 09 08 07 06
10 9 8 7 6 5 4 3 2 1

Library of Congress Cataloging-in-Publication Data
Parker, Victoria.
 The Titanic, 1912 / Vic Parker.
   p. cm. -- (When disaster struck)
 Includes bibliographical references and index.
 ISBN 1-4109-2282-0 (lib. bdg.)
 1. Titanic (Steamship)--Juvenile literature.
 2. Shipwrecks--North Atlantic Ocean--Juvenile
 literature. I. Title. II. Series.

 G530.T6P37 2006
 910.9163'4--dc22
                            2005034561

Acknowledgments
The publishers would like to thank the following for
permission to reproduce photographs:
AKG Images pp. 4, 38; Alamy Images pp. 12, 14,
25, 44 (Popperfoto/Getty Images); Bridgeman
Art Library p. 22; Corbis pp. 8 (Ralph White), 11,
24 (Bettmann/Underwood & Underwood), 31
(Bettmann), 36 (Matthew Polak), 39 (Hulton-
Deutsch Collection/Library of Congress), 43 (Jan
Butchofsky-Houser), 47 (Matthew Mcvay), 49
(Ralph White); Empics pp. 26, 42; Father Browne
Collection p. 21; Getty Images pp. 6, 9 (Robert
Welch/Sean Sexton), 19, 33, 41, 46, 48 (Michel
Boutefeu); John Frost Newspapers p. 40; Marconi
p. 29; Mary Evans Picture Library p. 35; The Picture
Desk p. 18 (Advertising Archives).

Cover illustration of the *Titanic* sinking, reproduced
with permission of Art Archive (Dagli Orti).

The publishers would like to thank Sheila Jemima
for her assistance in the preparation of this book.

CONTENTS

Any words appearing in the text in bold, **like this**, are explained in the glossary.

THE LOSS OF AN UNSINKABLE SHIP

The *Titanic*, 1912

A BRAND NEW SHIP

Imagine you are on board the biggest, most luxurious passenger ship in the world.

You are halfway between England and the United States, surrounded by the icy waters of the North Atlantic Ocean. It is nearly midnight. The sea is as smooth as a mirror. All is peaceful as the **liner** speeds along.

Suddenly it smashes against an enormous iceberg that is lurking in the darkness! A huge hole is made in the **hull**. Ice-cold water starts pouring in. In just a couple of hours, the ship will plunge to the bottom of the ocean. You are far from land, and there are not enough lifeboats.

Does this sound frightening? It is what happened to the passengers and crew on board the *Titanic* on April 14–15, 1912.

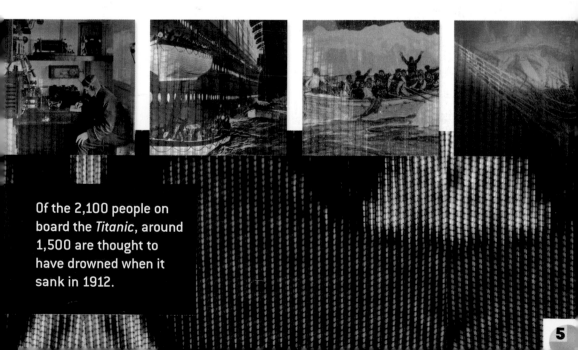

Of the 2,100 people on board the *Titanic*, around 1,500 are thought to have drowned when it sank in 1912.

THE BUILDING OF THE TITANIC

The *Titanic*, 1912

AN EXCITING WAY TO TRAVEL

Ocean liners were developed during the 1800s to take passengers speedily across oceans.

Many people from Europe wanted to travel to other **continents,** such as North America. Wealthy people wanted to go on exciting vacations. Many poorer people wanted to go abroad to make new lives for themselves. Other people wanted to travel on business.

Ship companies competed with each other to build the biggest, fastest, and most luxurious liners. Ocean liners became a glamorous and exciting way to travel.

In 1907 Lord William Pirrie and Bruce Ismay of the White Star Line drew up plans to build the three most magnificent ships in the world. They would be called the *Gigantic*, the *Olympic*, and the *Titanic*.

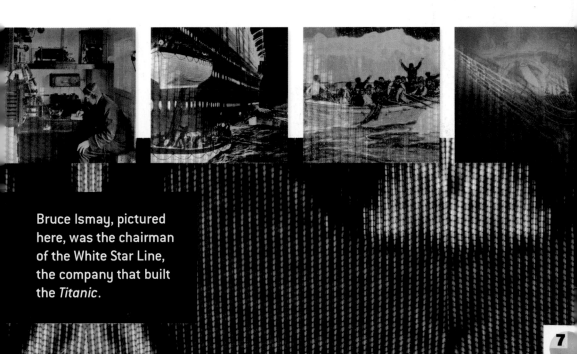

Bruce Ismay, pictured here, was the chairman of the White Star Line, the company that built the *Titanic*.

WORK BEGINS

The shipbuilders Harland & Wolff made ships for the White Star Line. Harland & Wolff's **shipyard** was in Belfast, Northern Ireland. Building the *Gigantic*, the *Olympic*, and the *Titanic* was a huge challenge.

At the time, the *Titanic* and the *Olympic* were the biggest ships ever built. Around three million **rivets** were used to build each liner.

Work began on the *Olympic* on December 16, 1908. Work on the *Titanic* began three months later, on March 31, 1909. The *Gigantic* was to be built later. The size of the liners meant that Harland & Wolff faced many difficulties. For instance the ships could not be built in the existing **slipways** because the slipways were too small. New slipways had to be built especially for these three ships.

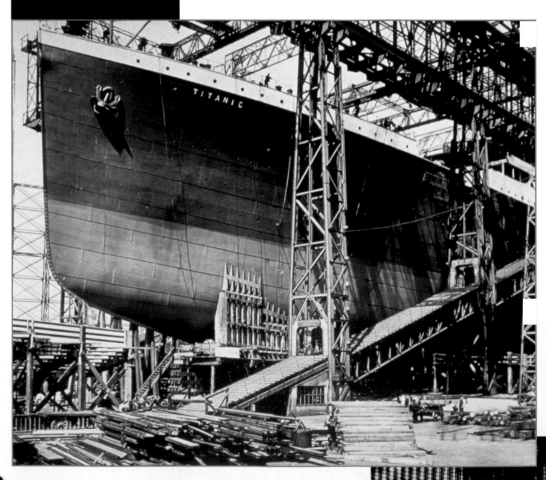

The first job was to position the **keels** of each ship. The framework of each ship was then built on top. The workers used a specially built scaffold called a gantry. Each gantry had a main crane fixed at the center. Other cranes could be moved to different parts of the gantry.

In the early 1900s, shipbuilding provided many jobs and made Belfast a thriving city.

Harland & Wolff was Belfast's biggest employer. The usual number of workers at the shipyard was about 6,000 people. However, the company had to take on another 6,000 workers to build the new liners. Most of the 12,000 workers lived in the streets near the shipyard. They were a proud team, and they were very careful with the massive ships they were building. Every day their hammering and drilling rang out around the docks. The whole city looked forward to admiring the finished ships.

A RECORD-BREAKING LINER

One of the White Star Line's major competitors was the Cunard Line. The pride of the Cunard Line were two liners called the *Mauretania* and the *Lusitania*. The *Mauretania* made its **maiden voyage** across the Atlantic Ocean in 1907. In 1909 it traveled across the Atlantic in just 4 days, 10 hours, and 51 minutes. Its average speed was 26.6 knots. This set a new record for the crossing.

A FAIL-SAFE DESIGN?

The hulls of each of the new ships were designed to have fifteen wall-like partitions to divide them into compartments. These partitions were called **bulkheads**. They were designed to increase safety. If a ship had a collision that ripped a hole in the hull, water would only fill the compartment behind the hole. The partitions would stop the water from filling the hull. This way, the ship would remain light enough to stay afloat. The ship would only sink if water flooded through the hull.

However, there were two problems with the design. First, the bulkheads had doors. If the doors were open, water could still flow through the hull. Second, there was a gap at the top of the bulkheads. If water filled one compartment, it could pour over the top of the bulkheads into the compartments on either side.

Fifteen bulkheads separated the hull of the *Titanic* into sixteen compartments.

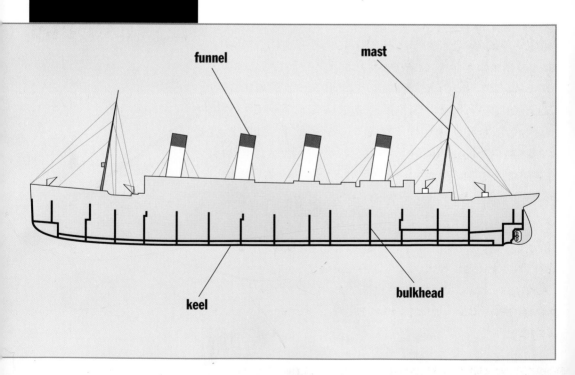

funnel

mast

keel

bulkhead

Harland & Wolff did not realize the dangers. They claimed that the bulkheads made their ships virtually unsinkable.

Nearly two years after work began on the *Olympic*, the hull, engines, and boilers were in place. The liner was ready to go into the water. Once in the water, the insides of the ship would be decorated. The *Olympic* was launched down the slipway on October 20, 1910. Thousands of people gathered on the dockside. They cheered as the enormous liner slid into the water. Grand celebrations were held to mark the event.

Not long afterward, on May 31, 1911, it was the *Titanic*'s turn. The occasion was even more exciting. The *Titanic* was going to be decorated and equipped even more **lavishly** than the *Olympic*. The *Titanic* was going to be the finest, heaviest, and most luxurious ship afloat.

PREPARING FOR PASSENGERS

The *Titanic*, 1912

FINISHING THE SHIP

After the *Titanic* was launched, tug boats towed the liner to the dockside.

Months of hard work could then begin to get the ship ready for passengers. The *Titanic* had eight passenger decks. Most of the top four decks were for first-class passengers only. These would be extremely wealthy people who expected to travel in luxury. The White Star Line spent large amounts of money to turn these decks into a floating palace! There were thick carpets, sculpted bronze railings, and enormous crystal **chandeliers**.

The ship also needed supplies, such as soap, bed linen, and writing paper. All of these items were made especially for the *Titanic*. Many companies were proud to supply items for the ship and boasted about it in their advertisements.

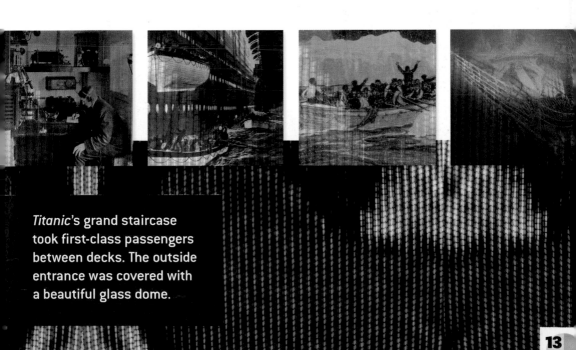

Titanic's grand staircase took first-class passengers between decks. The outside entrance was covered with a beautiful glass dome.

THE PASSENGERS' ROOMS

> "My pretty little cabin with its electric heater and pink curtains delighted me [...] its beautiful lace quilt and pink cushions and photographs all round [...] it all looked so homely [homey]." Lady Duff-Gordon, a first-class passenger.

The *Titanic* could carry 689 first-class passengers. First-class tickets cost from about $125. This would be thousands of dollars today. First-class cabins were called staterooms. There were different sizes and styles of stateroom. The two most expensive staterooms each had a sitting room, two bedrooms, two dressing rooms, a bathroom, and a private area of deck. Each cost $4,246 for a one-way voyage across the Atlantic. At the time this was an average person's earnings for twenty years! Many first-class passengers were millionaires who could afford the cost.

The White Star Line made sure that the first-class passengers were entertained throughout the voyage. There was a gym, a squash court, a swimming pool, a **Turkish bath**, a library, a magnificent dining room, and a variety of restaurants, bars, and lounges. First-class passengers could also walk on the top decks at the front of the ship. These areas were called **promenades**. There were three elevators to take them up and down from their cabins.

The finest rooms on the *Titanic* were as comfortable as those in the best hotels.

The *Titanic* could carry 674 second-class passengers. Most second-class passengers were people with well-paid jobs, such as lawyers, doctors, and **merchants**. A second-class ticket cost from $66 one way. This would be hundreds of dollars today. The second-class passengers on the *Titanic* had greater luxury than first-class passengers on many other ships! They had a grand dining room, a library, and several elegant bars and lounges. Their cabins were fitted with beautiful polished furniture. Each cabin slept two to four passengers. Second-class passengers had their own promenade and one elevator near the **stern** of the ship.

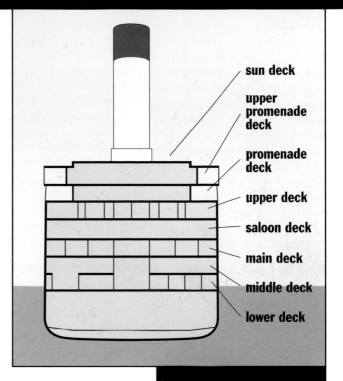

This cross section shows the deck levels inside the *Titanic*. The lowest deck, underneath the waterline, was where the boiler, engine, and mail rooms were housed.

The *Titanic* could also carry 1,026 third-class passengers. These would be poorer people, such as factory workers, farmworkers, and store clerks. A third-class ticket cost $36.25 one way. This was about two months' salary. Third-class cabins were much more basic than second-class cabins. However, the cabins all had running water, which many third-class passengers could not afford at home. There were cabins for families, cabins near the stern for women traveling alone to share, and a large **dormitory** in the **bow** of the ship for men traveling alone. Third-class was also known as steerage.

THE FINISHING TOUCHES

While the inside of the ship was being decorated, the outside of the ship was also being finished. Workers used an enormous floating crane to fix everything in place. Huge **funnels** were added through which smoke and steam from the boilers and engines could escape. Each funnel towered 175 feet (53 meters) from the *Titanic*'s keel. There were also two enormous **masts**. These were about 100 feet (30 meters) high. The masts were to be used as flagpoles and to support the **antennas** for the ship's radio communications system. The shipyard workers also had to attach the three huge **propellers** that would drive the liner through the sea. Made of bronze, the two biggest propellers were 23.5 feet (7 meters) wide.

Other workers constructed the buildings on the upper deck. These buildings included the room from which the captain and officers commanded the ship, called the bridge. The ship was steered from a room called the wheelhouse. The officers' quarters, where the officers rested and slept, were also built on the upper deck.

TITANIC'S STATISTICS

Length: 882 feet (269 meters). This is as long as 22 buses placed end to end.

Width: 92 feet (28 meters)

Height: 175 feet (53 meters)

Weight: 66,000 tons (fully laden)

Power: 50,000 **horsepower**

Cruising speed: 21 knots

Capacity: 3,547 passengers and crew

Lifeboat capacity: 1,178 people

Cost: $7,500,000

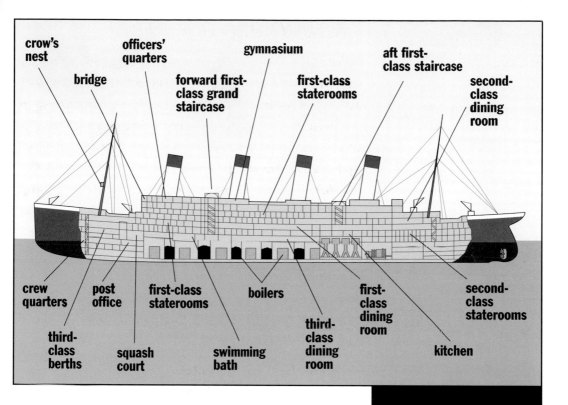

crow's nest

officers' quarters

gymnasium

aft first-class staircase

bridge

forward first-class grand staircase

first-class staterooms

second-class dining room

crew quarters

post office

first-class staterooms

boilers

first-class dining room

second-class staterooms

third-class berths

squash court

swimming bath

third-class dining room

kitchen

The *Titanic* also had to be fitted with lifeboats. At the time, the British Board of Trade rules said that the largest ships had to have sixteen lifeboats. Therefore, the *Titanic* had sixteen wooden lifeboats fixed to the upper deck. It also had four extra lifeboats. These had cloth sides so they could be collapsed and stored away. Of the wooden lifeboats, fourteen could each carry 65 people and two could each carry 40 people. The collapsible lifeboats could each carry 47 people.

However, the British Board of Trade rules were eighteen years old. The *Titanic* was four times bigger than the largest ship mentioned in the rules. The *Titanic* was not fitted with enough lifeboats to carry all the passengers and crew. The ship was built for 3,547 people, but the lifeboats could only carry 1,178.

The *Titanic* could comfortably accommodate 3,500 people.

AN UNEXPECTED DELAY

In June 1911, while the *Titanic* was being finished, the *Olympic* made its maiden voyage. The enormous ship was a success with passengers. By September it had made four trips between Southampton, England, and New York. But on the fifth trip, the *Olympic* collided with a warship, HMS *Hawke*. Nobody was injured, but the *Olympic* was damaged. It had to return to Belfast for repairs. The White Star Line had planned the *Titanic*'s maiden voyage for March 20, 1912, but work had to stop on the *Titanic* for two months while the shipyard crews worked on the *Olympic*. The *Titanic*'s maiden voyage was **postponed** until April 10. An advertisement was placed in *The Times* newspaper in England to announce the important occasion.

THE BUILDING OF THE TITANIC AND THE OLYMPIC

1907: White Star Line plans the *Gigantic*, the *Olympic*, and the *Titanic*.

December 16, 1908: Work begins on the *Olympic*.

March 31, 1909: Work begins on the *Titanic*.

October 20, 1910: The *Olympic* is launched into the water for fitting-out.

May 31, 1911: The *Titanic* is launched into the water for fitting-out.

June 14, 1911: The *Olympic* makes its maiden voyage.

Oct./Nov. 1911: Work stops on the *Titanic* while the *Olympic* is repaired after colliding with another ship.

April 2, 1912: The *Titanic*'s sea trials are carried out.

April 10, 1912: The *Titanic* makes its maiden voyage.

Posters such as this one advertised the *Titanic*'s maiden voyage.

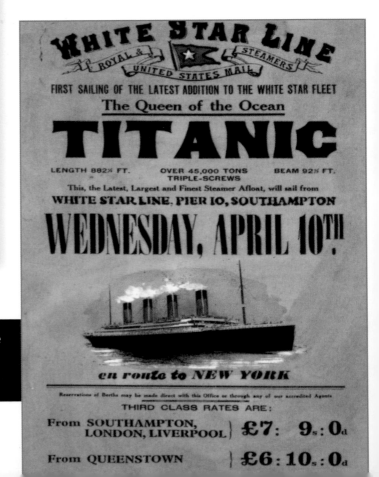

WHITE STAR LINE
ROYAL & STEAMERS
UNITED STATES MAIL

FIRST SAILING OF THE LATEST ADDITION TO THE WHITE STAR FLEET

The Queen of the Ocean

TITANIC

LENGTH 882½ FT. OVER 45,000 TONS TRIPLE-SCREWS BEAM 92½ FT.

This, the Latest, Largest and Finest Steamer Afloat, will sail from

WHITE STAR LINE, PIER 10, SOUTHAMPTON

WEDNESDAY, APRIL 10TH

en route to NEW YORK

Reservations of Berths may be made direct with this Office or through any of our accredited Agents

THIRD CLASS RATES ARE:

From SOUTHAMPTON, LONDON, LIVERPOOL £7 : 9s : 0d

From QUEENSTOWN £6 : 10s : 0d

All ships have to be trialed (tested) at sea before they are allowed to carry passengers. The *Titanic*'s sea trials were set for Monday, April 1, 1912. Throughout March, crew members arrived at the shipyard. Everyone had to learn about the ship and their duties on board.

The day of the trial arrived. However, the tests had to be put off because of bad weather. Finally, the following morning, tug boats pulled the *Titanic* out to sea. The ship's engines were fired up and the *Titanic* steamed away for the first time.

Tests were carried out all day. An official from the British Board of Trade watched carefully. Many companies that had made equipment for the *Titanic* also sent inspectors. They made sure that everything was working properly. At last, everyone was satisfied. The Board of Trade official issued a certificate that said the *Titanic* was safe and ready for passengers. At 8:00 P.M. the *Titanic* set off for Southampton, the starting point for its maiden voyage.

The *Titanic*'s sea trials included **maneuvers,** such as tight turns and emergency stops. Controlling and steering such an enormous ship was a difficult job.

A HURRY TO LOAD THE SHIP

The *Titanic* arrived at Southampton just after 12:00 A.M. on Thursday, April 4. Over the next seven days, the ship was stocked for its voyage. Huge crates of supplies were delivered to the docks for loading. There were huge quantities of food, bedding, towels, crockery, and cutlery. Many tons of coal were stored on board to fuel the engines. The *Titanic* would also be carrying mail across the Atlantic. Sacks of letters and parcels were carried into the cargo hold. The ship's full title was RMS *Titanic*, or Royal Mail Ship *Titanic*.

The *Titanic* had arrived in Southampton a day later than planned because the sea trials had been delayed. Everyone had to work quickly to get the liner ready to leave on time. There were still plenty of last-minute jobs to do, such as touching up paintwork and arranging furniture. The docks were buzzing with activity and excitement.

Early in the morning on Wednesday, April 10, hundreds of crew members boarded the *Titanic*. Between 9:30 A.M. and 11:30 A.M., trains bringing passengers from London arrived. Many of the third-class passengers and some second-class passengers were traveling one way. They were going to the United States to start a new life. Third-class passengers carried just one or two bags.

Meanwhile, first-class passengers arrived with many suitcases and trunks. Some brought their maid or butler. Others paid for their dogs to travel in the ship's kennel area. One passenger even paid for his car to be carried in the cargo hold. For many first-class passengers, the trip was to be an enjoyable and fashionable vacation.

Not everyone planning to travel on the *Titanic* ended up boarding the ship. Twenty-two crew members failed to arrive on time. Fifty-five passengers canceled their bookings at the last moment. In total, over 900 passengers boarded the ship. The youngest was Millvina Dean, who was just nine weeks old.

Mail and trunks were brought to the *Titanic* on board **tenders,** such as this one.

At last, the *Titanic* was ready for its maiden voyage.

FULL STEAM AHEAD!

The *Titanic*, 1912

OUT TO SEA

At noon on April 10, 1912, the world's largest and most luxurious liner began its maiden voyage.

The dockside was packed with people cheering as tug boats pulled the ship down the Test River toward the sea. The excited passengers crowded the rails, waving to their family and friends.

Soon the *Titanic* was out in the open sea. First, it traveled to Cherbourg, France. Some passengers were only traveling to France and left the ship there. Three-hundred new passengers came on board. On April 11, it stopped at Queenstown, Ireland. Again, some passengers left the ship, and over 100 new passengers came on board. Finally, the *Titanic* steamed away into the Atlantic Ocean.

Crowds of people lined the dockside to watch the *Titanic* set off on its maiden voyage.

THE CREW GETS BUSY

The *Titanic*'s crew members soon settled into their daily routines. The crew contained nearly 900 men and women. They were headed by Captain Edward Smith and his seven commanding officers: Chief Officer Henry Wilde, First Officer William Murdoch, Second Officer Charles Lightoller, Third Officer Herbert Pitman, Fourth Officer Joseph Boxhall, Fifth Officer Harold Lowe, and Sixth Officer James Moody.

Nearly 500 crew members looked after the passengers. These included stewards and stewardesses, restaurant managers, chefs, waiters and waitresses, room maids, laundry staff, cleaners, barbers, swimming pool attendants, and store clerks.

"It is difficult to convey any idea of the size of a ship like the *Titanic*, when you could actually walk miles along decks and passages, covering different ground all the time [...] it took me fourteen days before I could with confidence find my way from one part of that ship to another by the shortest route."

Commander Lightoller (Second Officer on the ship).

First-class passengers enjoyed grand meals in the main dining room of the *Titanic*.

Around 400 crew members had other duties. These included the ship's engineers and sailors, boiler room workers, and mail room staff.

No one knows exactly how many people were on board the *Titanic*. However, we know that there were over 1,300 passengers. There were about 325 passengers in first class, about 285 in second class, and about 700 in third class.

There was plenty for first- and second-class passengers to do. Many used the indoor facilities, such as the libraries, or played board games, such as chess and backgammon. People also took photographs, wrote letters and diaries, and chatted with other passengers. Outdoors, people could relax in deckchairs and play games, such as **ring toss**. Musicians played in different public rooms around the ship.

The evening meal was the highlight of the day for first-class passengers. They dressed in fine clothes and enjoyed a seven-course meal. Afterward they danced or chatted. Dinner in second class was a special event, too, with a delicious four-course meal. Third-class dinners were much simpler, but the food was tasty and filling. The third-class dining room had space for only around 470 people, so third-class passengers were given tickets to eat at different times.

Third-class passengers had the least to do on board. There were two rooms where they could play cards, chat, or sing and dance. They could also stroll on deck, but only at the back of the ship. It was often very smoky there, since smoke from the funnels trailed back over the ship.

First-class passengers enjoyed strolling on deck and taking in the ocean views.

ICE WARNINGS

The *Titanic* steamed west into the cold waters of the North Atlantic. Each day Captain Smith increased the ship's speed. This may have been because Bruce Ismay, the White Star Line chairman, was on board. It is thought that he urged Captain Smith to go faster because he wanted to arrive early in New York. Ismay would have wanted to show everyone that the *Titanic* was fast as well as luxurious. By Sunday, April 14, Captain Smith had ordered 24 of the *Titanic*'s 29 boilers to blaze away. The heat and noise in the boiler rooms was almost unbearable. The ship raced along at 22.5 knots.

This photo is possibly of the actual iceberg the *Titanic* hit. It was taken six days after the disaster by F. H. Lardner, captain of the *Mackay-Bennett*.

The *Titanic* had two radio operators: John Phillips and Harold Bride. Each day they picked up warnings from other ships about an area of floating ice and icebergs. On April 14 they received seven warnings. They took most of them straight to the captain and officers on the bridge. However, the two radio operators were extremely busy. They had lots of messages to send from the *Titanic*'s passengers to people on shore. They did not deliver all of the warnings to the bridge.

Captain Smith and the officers thought that the *Titanic* would reach the area of ice between 10:00 P.M. and 12:00 A.M. However, the captain did not seem to be worried. Maybe he thought there would be plenty of time to spot any danger. Captain Smith did not slow down the ship or post extra lookouts.

At 7:00 P.M. Captain Smith went to a dinner party. At 9:00 P.M. he checked on his officers on the bridge. Half an hour later he retired to his cabin. At 9:45 P.M. one of the officers, James Moody, spoke to the two lookouts, Frederick Fleet and Reginald Lee. He told them to keep an eye out for ice.

At 10:00 P.M. a ship called the *Rappahannock* passed the *Titanic* going in the opposite direction. It used signal lamps to flash the message, "Have just passed through heavy ice field and several icebergs." The *Titanic*'s officers replied, "Message received. Thanks. Goodnight." The ship continued into the darkness.

TITANIC'S MORSE CODE MESSAGES

At the time the use of radio on board ships was quite new. Radio operators used a system called Morse Code. Combinations of long and short beeps stood for different letters and numbers. The operators' job was mainly to deal with messages between passengers and people on shore, rather than to communicate with other ships.

DISASTER STRIKES!

The *Titanic*, 1912

200—26/4/12   MIMCC 6

Forwarding Charges _____ COPY Delivered or sent date _apl 15_

SERVICE FORM.

THE MARCONI INTERNATIONAL MARINE COMMUNICATION Co. Ltd.

Office Rec'd from	Time Rec'd	By whom Received	Office sent to	Time Sent	By whom Sent
	m.				m.

No. _1_   OFFICE _apl 15_ 191_

Prefix _____ Code _____ Words _____

From _Titanic_ To _Cqd_

Position 41.46 N 50.14 W

require assistance

struck iceberg

DANGER IN THE DARKNESS

Up in the crow's nest, the lookouts were peering into the darkness, straining to see any sign of ice.

They did not have **binoculars** because officers could not find any on board. It was a cloudy night and the sea was calm. It was hard for them to see anything.

At 11:40 P.M. Fleet thought he saw a huge shape straight in front of the ship. He rang the warning bell and telephoned the bridge. "Iceberg, right ahead!" he warned. First Officer William Murdoch, who was in charge of the ship at that time, pressed a control to shut the doors in the bulkheads. He gave orders to turn the ship, but as the ship tried to steer around the iceberg, there was a jolt. Enormous chunks of ice fell onto a lower deck. The side of the *Titanic* had scraped along the iceberg.

The *Titanic*'s distress signal gave the ship's position and requested assistance from nearby ships.

CONFUSION

In his cabin Captain Smith felt the ship shudder. He dashed to the bridge and sent Fourth Officer Joseph Boxhall to inspect the damage. Boxhall went down to the third-class decks, but did not find any problems. It seemed as though the *Titanic* had narrowly avoided disaster. However, the ship's carpenter soon arrived on the bridge in a panic. He was closely followed by a terrified mail room worker. They both reported that the hull was filling with water.

In fact, a line of jagged holes stretched along the ship below the waterline. The collision had punctured six of the hull's compartments. Freezing-cold seawater was gushing into the boiler and mail rooms. The horrified workers were half-wading, half-swimming to get out.

Captain Smith summoned Thomas Andrews to the bridge. Andrews was managing director of Harland & Wolff. Together they went to find out how bad the damage was. Andrews realized that water was going to flood through many compartments of the hull. This would make the ship too heavy to stay afloat. Andrews estimated that the *Titanic* had, at most, only two hours left before it sank.

PASSENGER REACTIONS

Most people on the *Titanic* did not realize that anything was wrong. When the ship hit the iceberg, the first- and second-class passengers on the upper decks felt only a rumble and a tremble. Some enjoyed watching the iceberg go past their windows. Many were asleep and did not wake up. Crew members and third-class passengers in the cabins nearest the collision felt it more strongly. However, they did not fully understand what had happened.

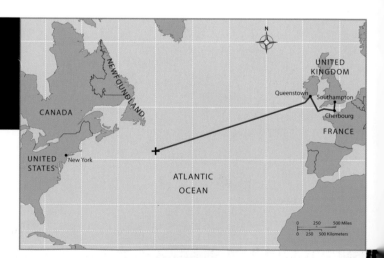

The *Titanic* was nearing the end of its journey when it hit the iceberg.

The *Titanic*'s distress signals were first picked up in the wireless room of the SS *Carpathia*.

Captain Smith took the ship's position to the radio operators, who began to send messages for help. They used two distress signals, CQD (the distress signal commonly used at the time) and SOS (a new distress signal).

At least five ships picked up the signals. A Cunard liner called the *Carpathia* was the closest. It was carrying passengers from New York to the Mediterranean Sea. However, it was still about four hours away. Its captain, Arthur Rostron, ordered the crew to head for the *Titanic* at full speed.

Captain Smith and Fourth Officer Boxhall spotted the lights of another ship nearby. They used signaling lamps to flash the CQD distress signal. However, the lights faded as the ship passed. No one has ever discovered the identity of this ship. For many years, people thought it was a ship called the *Californian* and that its crew ignored the *Titanic*'s distress flares. Many people now think the crew of the *Californian* was hunting seals. This is illegal, which might explain why the ship did not stop.

ABANDON SHIP!

Stewards banged on the cabin doors. They told everyone to put on life jackets and get ready to board the lifeboats.

The first-and second-class passengers were the first on deck. They saw Fourth Officer Boxhall firing rocket distress signals into the sky. They were stunned at what was happening.

TROUBLE IN THIRD CLASS

It took the third-class passengers a long time to arrive on deck. They had to come from the lower levels of the ship. They had to walk through the rising, freezing water. Many had to break through the gates that shut off second- and first-class areas.

There had not been a lifeboat drill since the ship left Southampton. Although the *Titanic*'s officers were experienced, they seemed unsure what to do. They had never seen an emergency like this. The lifeboats could be lowered by ropes and pulleys into the water, but the officers worried that the lifeboats would buckle if they were full of passengers when lowered. There were several Harland & Wolff workers on board who knew this would not happen, but none of them said anything. So, the officers allowed only a few passengers into each lifeboat. It should have been possible for more passengers to board once the lifeboats were in the water, through hatches (small doors) in lower decks. However, the *Titanic* was already sinking lower in the sea, and the escape hatches had fallen below the waterline. They could not be opened.

The officers followed a rule that said women and children had **priority** over men. At first many people refused to get in. They did not want to leave the huge, comfortable *Titanic* for a small, wooden boat.

At 12:45 A.M. the first lifeboat was lowered down the side of the ship. It was designed for 65 people, but only 28 people were on board. Over the next 30 minutes, three more lifeboats were lowered. They carried just 36, 28, and 32 passengers each.

As more lifeboats left, it became clear that there would not be enough boats to hold all the passengers. Now, the deck was slanting as the *Titanic*'s bow sunk lower. People began to panic. Many started pushing and shoving, trying to get close to a lifeboat. A few people even jumped dangerously into lifeboats that were being lowered. Fifth Officer Lowe fired his gun into the air to try to prevent the crowds from rioting.

The GREATEST WRECK in HISTORY
THE LOSS OF THE WHITE STAR TITANIC
THE LARGEST SHIP IN THE WORLD, WHICH SANK ON ITS MAIDEN VOYAGE WITH A LOSS OF 1635 LIVES

LEAVING THE SINKING LINER: A PERILOUS MOMENT FOR THE LIFEBOATS

"'Stop lowering 14,' our crew shouted, and the crew of No. 14, now only 20 feet above, cried out the same. The distance to the top, however, was some seventy feet, and the creaking of the pulleys must have deadened all sound to those above, for down she came—fifteen feet, ten feet, five feet—and a stoker and I reached up and touched the bottom of the swinging boat above our heads. The next drop would have brought her on our heads. Just before she dropped, another stoker sprang to the ropes with his knife open in his hand. 'One,' I heard him say, and then 'Two,' as the knife cut through the pulley-ropes. The next moment the exhaust stream carried us clear."—Mr. Beesley's narrative.

This artist's impression shows the lifeboats being lowered into the water.

FACING THE END

Some passengers were offered a place in a lifeboat but chose not to go. Many were women, such as Ida Strauss, who would not leave their husbands. She stayed with her husband, Isidor, the wealthy owner of Macy's department store in New York. A priest named Father Thomas Byles chose to stay behind and lead people in prayers.

Other passengers were not offered a place in a lifeboat but remained calm. Millionaire Benjamin Guggenheim and his butler went to their cabin and put on their evening suits. He said, "We've dressed in our best and are prepared to go down like gentlemen." Some people went below deck to drink or play cards.

However, many people were desperate. Some tried to lash deckchairs together to make rafts. Despite the danger, many crew members kept doing their jobs to try to occupy people. The gym instructor even encouraged people to try the sports equipment. The band played cheerful tunes and rousing hymns.

At around 2:18 A.M., the weight of the water flooding the bow tipped the ship down toward the seabed. Water poured onto the decks. Hundreds of people were washed away, together with the last two collapsible lifeboats. The stern of the ship was lifted high into the air. Some passengers scrambled up the vertical deck; others fell screaming into the water. Under the strain the hull snapped between the back funnels. The bow section of *Titanic* was deep under water. At 2:20 A.M. the stern section, and everyone on it, sank.

TIMELINE OF THE ACCIDENT

April 14, 1912
11:40 P.M. The *Titanic* strikes an iceberg and begins to take on water.

April 15, 1912
12:30 A.M. Officers start loading passengers onto the lifeboats.

12:40 A.M. Captain Smith and Fourth Officer Boxhall flash distress signals to a passing ship, but it does not stop.

12:45 A.M. Fourth Officer Boxhall fires the first of eight rocket signals, which were sent up at five-minute intervals. The first lifeboat is lowered.

2:05 A.M. The eighteenth lifeboat is lowered. The last two lifeboats are washed away before they can be launched.

2:20 A.M. The *Titanic* sinks.

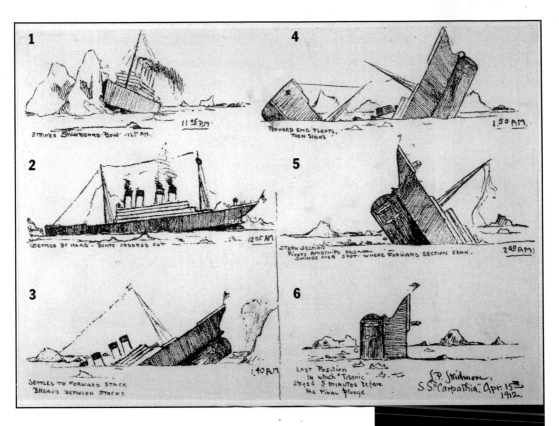

1 STRIKES STARBOARD BOW – 11.40 P.M.   11.40 P.M.

2 SETTLES BY HEAD – BOATS ORDERED OUT   12.05 A.M.

3 SETTLES TO FORWARD STACK
BREAKS BETWEEN STACKS   1.40 A.M.

4 FORWARD END FLOATS,
THEN SINKS   1.50 A.M.

5 STERN SECTION
PIVOTS AMIDSHIPS AND
SWINGS OVER SPOT WHERE FORWARD SECTION SANK.   2.00 A.M.

6 LAST POSITION
IN WHICH "Titanic"
STAYED 5 MINUTES BEFORE
THE FINAL PLUNGE   L.P. Skidmore,
S.S. "Carpathia" Apr. 15th
1912.

These drawings show the stages of the sinking of the *Titanic*. They are based on the sketches of a passenger named John Thayer, who saw the sinking from a lifeboat.

"As she swung up, her lights, which had shone without a flicker all night, went out suddenly, came on again for a single flash, then went out altogether. And as they did so, there came a noise [...] it was partly a roar, partly a groan, partly a rattle, and partly a smash [...] as the heavy machinery dropped down to the bottom (now the bows) of the ship [...] When the noise was over the *Titanic* was still upright like a column [...] then [...] she slid slowly forwards through the water and dived slantingly down; the sea closed over her."

Lawrence Beesley, a second-class passenger.

THE RESCUE

The *Titanic*, 1912

IN THE LIFEBOATS

By this time, more than 700 passengers were adrift in the lifeboats.

Hundreds more were struggling in the water, crying out for help. Only one lifeboat, commanded by Fifth Officer Lowe, went back to help. The passengers pulled four people from the ocean. Other lifeboats turned people away. Many passengers were terrified that the boats would become overcrowded and sink. Other lifeboats were partly flooded and already in danger of sinking.

Around 50 people scrambled onto the two collapsible lifeboats that had been washed off the *Titanic*'s deck. However, one was filled with icy water and the other was upside down.

During the night, many lifeboat passengers died of the cold, or they became unable to cling onto their boats and drowned. All those left in the freezing water died.

Many of the *Titanic*'s lifeboats could have carried more survivors.

A RACE TO SAVE LIVES

Meanwhile, Captain Rostron was doing everything he could to make the *Carpathia* go as fast as possible. He also prepared for the *Titanic*'s passengers. He ordered lifeboats to be readied. He had ladders dropped down the side of the ship. He had first-aid stations set up. He organized his own passengers to be ready with blankets, warm clothing, hot drinks, soup, and sandwiches. The captain also posted extra lookouts. They were to watch for icebergs as well as any sign of the *Titanic* or people in the water.

The crew and passengers of the *Carpathia* only discovered that the *Titanic* had sunk when they rescued the lifeboat passengers.

At 3:30 A.M. the *Carpathia* arrived at the location given by the *Titanic*. No one on board could see anything except ice. For half an hour, everyone searched in the darkness. Then, suddenly they saw a dim light below them. It was a flare from a lifeboat. The passengers, led by Fourth Officer Boxhall, rowed as hard as they could to the big liner. Some climbed on board. Others had to be pulled up on ropes. Many cried with shock and relief.

Survivors gathered on the *Carpathia's* deck. Many of them mistakenly believed that other ships had rescued their friends and family.

It took more than four hours for the *Carpathia* to pick up all the survivors. The big ship could not steam to the lifeboats because of the ice. Instead, the lifeboats had to row to the liner. By this time, the lifeboats were scattered over about 4 miles (6.4 kilometers) of ocean.

At 8:30 A.M. the last lifeboat reached the *Carpathia*. At the same time, the *Californian* arrived to help. Soon after 9:00 A.M. the *Carpathia* set off for New York with about 700 survivors on board. The *Californian* stayed to search for more survivors, but no more were found.

TIMELINE OF THE RESCUE

April 15, 1912, 2:20 A.M.
The *Titanic* sinks.

4:00 A.M.
The *Carpathia* picks up the first survivors from the lifeboats.

8:30 A.M.
The last lifeboat reaches the *Carpathia*. The *Californian* arrives.

9:15 A.M.
The *Carpathia* sets off for New York.

April 18, 1912, 9:30 P.M.
The *Carpathia* arrives in New York.

THE NEWS BREAKS

By the early hours of Monday, April 15, the news that the *Titanic* had run into serious trouble had spread around the world. Radio operators in New York and in Newfoundland, Canada, had picked up the ship's faint distress signals. However, no one knew yet exactly what had happened.

During the day, a radio operator in Philadelphia picked up a message from the *Carpathia* to the *Titanic*'s sister ship, the *Olympic*. It was a list of names of survivors. Many different rumors began to spread. A newspaper organization called Associated Press contacted the *Carpathia* asking for information. However, the ship did not tell them anything. Captain Rostron wanted to make sure the owners of the *Titanic*, the White Star Line, knew all the details of the accident first.

Many newspapers went ahead and published reports anyway. Most were incorrect. The *Evening Sun* newspaper in New York printed that the *Titanic* had hit an iceberg, but that everybody was safe and the ship was being towed to Canada.

THE NEWS REACHES SOUTHAMPTON

"A great many girls have been absent this afternoon owing to the sad news regarding the *Titanic*. Fathers and brothers are on the vessel; and some of the little ones have been in tears all afternoon."

Teacher's entry in a local Southampton, England, school log, April 15, 1912.

The first reports of the collision suggested that the *Titanic* had not sunk.

The Evening Gazette

TITANIC RAMS ICEBERG; 1470 PASSENGERS SAFE

THE GIANT LINER TITANIC

HUMAN·FREIGHT TRANSFERRED TO CARPATHIA IN CALM SEAS

Giant Liner Still Afloat. Two Ships By Her Side. Olympic, Baltic and Others Nearing Scene. Officials Declare $10,000,000 Craft Cannot Sink

CLARA BARTON

W. C. PORTER ON WRECKED LINER

There was chaos and confusion at White Star Line offices on both sides of the Atlantic.

That evening, the *Olympic* sent a radio message confirming that the *Titanic* had sunk. Two hours later, the *Carpathia* radioed that it was bringing the survivors to New York.

Thousands of people gathered outside the White Star Line offices in New York and in Southampton, England. The family and friends of the *Titanic*'s crew and passengers were desperate for information. It was difficult for the White Star Line to get all the information it needed and be sure that details were accurate. Over the next couple of days, the company posted lists of survivors. However, some of the names were mixed up or spelled incorrectly. Some people were wrongly led to believe that their family and friends had survived.

SAFELY BACK ON LAND

The *Carpathia* finally arrived in New York harbor in the evening of Thursday, April 18. Many small boats went out to meet the ship. Some held family and friends of the survivors. Most held members of the press. They shouted questions to the survivors and tried to take photographs.

The *Carpathia* headed first for the White Star Line piers. There the *Titanic*'s lifeboats were lowered back into the water. Then the liner went to the piers of its own company, Cunard. By 9:30 P.M. it was anchored. Gradually the survivors were led off the ship. Once again, they were approached by members of the press, desperate for comments and pictures. Some survivors went to their homes in the city or to hotels. Others were taken to the hospital because they were suffering from shock, **frostbite**, or injuries such as broken bones. Many of the third-class survivors had nowhere to go and no money.

A SAD MYSTERY IS SOLVED

One of the bodies recovered by the *Mackay-Bennett* was a baby boy. Nobody could find out who he was. Lots of people offered to pay for his funeral, but the captain and crew of the *Mackay-Bennett* insisted that they pay for it. In 2002 experts at Canada's Lakehead University ran tests on the body. They traced the child to a family in Finland who had lost relatives in the disaster. They discovered that the boy had been thirteen months old and named Eino Viljami Panula.

The crew members of this small boat are from one of the ships sent to recover the dead of the *Titanic* disaster. They are pulling a body wearing a life jacket from the water.

The White Star Line paid for several Canadian ships to look for the dead. The *Mackay-Bennett* was the first to reach the area where the ship had sunk. It arrived in the evening of Saturday, April 20. Within six days, the crew had recovered 306 bodies from the sea. The *Minia*, the *Montmagny*, and the *Algerine* found more. The last bodies were found accidentally. One month after the disaster, a liner called the *Oceanic* came across one of the collapsible lifeboats. It was adrift and contained three bodies. In all 328 bodies were found.

Many of the bodies were too badly damaged to be identified. These bodies were **buried at sea**. The rest were taken to Halifax, Canada. Some were claimed by relatives and friends, who took the coffins away for burial. However, it proved too difficult to identify many of the dead. These bodies were buried in Halifax.

Most of the recovered victims of the *Titanic* disaster are buried in Fairview Cemetery in Halifax, Canada.

THE TITANIC'S LEGACY

The *Titanic*, 1912

THE INQUIRIES BEGIN

The U.S. government began an inquiry (investigation) into the disaster just five days after the sinking.

A British inquiry began on May 2, 1912. Many experts, as well as passengers and officers from the ships involved, gave evidence.

The U.S. inquiry found that Captain Smith had been over-confident, **indifferent** to danger, and had neglected his duties. The inquiry blamed Captain Smith for taking unnecessary risks. It also blamed the British Board of Trade for poor safety standards. The British inquiry blamed both Captain Smith and the design of the *Titanic*'s bulkheads. The inquiries also found that the *Californian* had not been far from the *Titanic* when it sank. However, it had not picked up the *Titanic*'s distress signals because the radio operator had gone to bed. At the time a ship's radio did not have to be manned 24 hours a day.

The actions of some of the *Titanic*'s officers, including Captain Smith (right), were questioned by the inquiries.

THE RECOMMENDATIONS

Both inquiries recommended important changes. The recommendations were intended to prevent another similar disaster from happening. The inquiries said that every ship should have a good quality radio system, manned 24 hours a day. Every ship should carry enough lifeboats for everyone on board and hold regular lifeboat drills. The inquiries also said that ships should always slow down when approaching icy areas. They said that ships should take a more southerly route across the Atlantic Ocean, where there was less of a chance of meeting big icebergs.

THE LOSS OF LIFE

Many more first- and second-class passengers were saved than third-class passengers and crew. Many questions were raised about who should have been given priority. The exact numbers of passengers and crew on board the *Titanic* have never been officially established. These figures are from the U.S. inquiry:

First class:
199 people saved
130 people lost

Second class:
119 people saved
166 people lost

Third class:
174 people saved
536 people lost

Crew:
214 people saved
685 people lost

This poster advertised tickets for a journey that never happened—the return sailing of the *Titanic* from New York to the United Kingdom.

Modern ships now do all of these things. There have been many efforts to improve bulkhead design, too. The *Titanic* disaster has shown everyone that no ship is unsinkable.

Another result of the disaster was the International Ice Patrol Service. Set up in 1914, the service is still in operation today. It is a group of scientists from sixteen countries around the North Atlantic. The scientists' main job is to track and report icebergs so that they can warn ships. However, they also carry out research into icebergs to find out more about how they form and how they behave.

The scientists use airplanes to drop **buoys** into icy areas. The buoys contain computers that take measurements, such as the temperature of the sea and the direction of the waves. They then send this information back to the scientists. The scientists can use the information to figure out where icebergs are likely to appear and how big they are likely to be.

The International Ice Patrol service has saved many lives. Here workers are preparing a satellite buoy to be dropped in the ocean.

DISCOVERING THE WRECK

Ever since the *Titanic* sank, people have wanted to find the ship and raise it from the bottom of the ocean. Among the first people to suggest plans for this were a group of wealthy *Titanic* survivors. However, the plans eventually came to nothing. Since then many other people have tried to find the wreck but failed.

People began to wonder if the *Titanic* had perhaps disintegrated (broken apart) under the water, or maybe it had been buried by an undersea earthquake. Even if the wreck were found, experts did not know if it could be recovered.

It looked as if the *Titanic* would never be seen again. But just after 12:00 A.M. on September 1, 1985, a group of U.S. and French scientists found it. The scientists had been searching the seabed with an unmanned **submersible** called *Argo*, which sent pictures back to their ship.

These items are among hundreds of objects **salvaged** from the wreck of the *Titanic*.

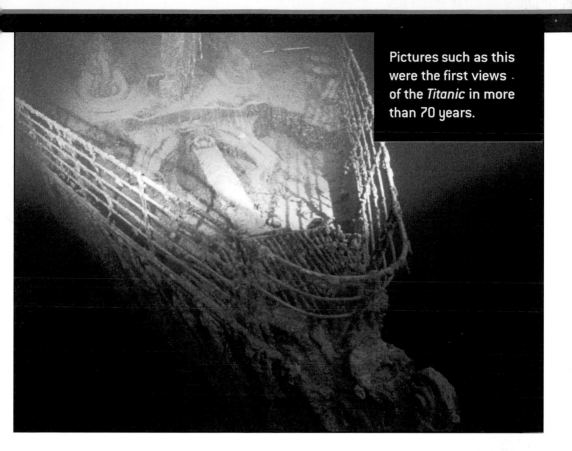

Pictures such as this were the first views of the *Titanic* in more than 70 years.

Since then there have been expeditions to explore the wreck. It is rusty from the seawater, but many objects are still intact. Some items, such as plates, bits of coal, passengers' clothes, and light fixtures, have been brought to the surface. Many people want to recover all the ship's contents and the ship itself, if possible. They feel it is a fascinating piece of history that should be put on display. However, many other people think that the ship is a graveyard and should be left undisturbed.

Every year on the anniversary of the sinking, an airplane flies over it and drops a wreath. This ceremony is to remember all the people who died.

THE TITANIC BECOMES A LEGEND

The story of the *Titanic* has been told in books, movies, plays, and songs. Some of these have stuck to the facts, while others have changed parts of the story. One film version of the *Titanic* story was released in 1997. It was directed by James Cameron and starred Kate Winslet and Leonardo DiCaprio. It won eleven Oscars and became the most successful movie of all time.

TIMELINE

1907 The White Star Line plans to construct three massive liners: the *Gigantic*, the *Olympic*, and the *Titanic*.

March 31, 1909 Work starts on the *Titanic* in Belfast, Northern Ireland.

May 31, 1911 The *Titanic* is launched and fitting-out begins.

April 4, 1912 The *Titanic* arrives at Southampton, England.

April 10, 1912 **12:00 P.M.** The *Titanic* leaves Southampton on its maiden voyage.

6:30 P.M. The *Titanic* arrives in Cherbourg, France.

8:30 P.M. The ship leaves Cherbourg.

April 11, 1912 The *Titanic* stops at Queenstown, Ireland.

1:30 P.M. The ship leaves for New York.

April 14, 1912 The *Titanic* receives ice warnings from other ships throughout the day and evening.

9:30 P.M. Captain Smith retires to his cabin for the night.

11:40 P.M. The *Titanic*'s lookout, Frederick Fleet, spots an iceberg and informs the bridge. The *Titanic* hits the iceberg.

11:55 P.M. The ship's boiler rooms and mail rooms begin to flood.

April 15, 1912 **12:00 A.M.** Captain Smith orders the *Titanic*'s radio operators to send distress signals. He orders the lifeboats to be readied. He instructs stewards to prepare the passengers to abandon ship.

12:40 A.M. The lights of a passing ship are spotted and distress signals are flashed, but the ship passes by.

12:45 A.M. The first of eight distress rockets is sent up and the first lifeboat is launched.

1:20 A.M. The *Titanic*'s deck is sloping as the bow sinks lower into the water.

2:17 A.M. The *Titanic*'s bow sinks. Hundreds of people are washed away.

2:18 A.M. The *Titanic* rises vertically out of the water. The hull breaks in half.

2:20 A.M. The remaining stern section of the *Titanic* sinks from view.

3:30 A.M. The *Carpathia* arrives at the location of the sinking.

4:00 A.M. The crew of the *Carpathia* sees the first lifeboat.

8:30 A.M. The last lifeboat reaches the *Carpathia* just as the *Californian* arrives.

April 18, 1912 **9:30 P.M.** The survivors arrive in New York, on board the *Carpathia*.

April 19, 1912 An inquiry into the disaster begins in New York. It makes its report on May 28.

April 20, 1912 The first of several ships sent by White Star Line to find bodies of *Titanic*'s dead arrives in the area of the sinking.

May 2, 1912 An inquiry into the disaster begins in the United Kingdom. It reports on July 30, 1912.

Sept. 1, 1985 The wreck of *Titanic* is discovered.

GLOSSARY

antenna equipment made of metal used for sending and receiving radio and television signals

binoculars device that allows a person to see farther into the distance

bow front end of a ship

bulkhead upright partition separating two compartments

buoy floating object used as a marker in water—for instance, to mark out a shipping lane

buried at sea ceremony held on a ship in which a dead body is wrapped in sheets, weighted down, and tipped overboard

chandelier expensive light fixture made up of many glass pieces

continent one of the seven large ares that Earth's land is divided into

crow's nest platform high up on a ship's mast, where lookouts stand for a clear view of a wide area around a ship

dormitory room containing many beds

frostbite illness in which skin that has been freezing cold starts to rot and fall off

funnel chimney through which smoke leaves a ship

horsepower unit for measuring the power of engines

hull main body of a ship

indifferent showing no interest in something

keel heavy base of a ship that acts like its backbone

knots used to measure the speed of a boat. 1 knot = 1.2 miles (1.9 kilometers) per hour.

lavish having more than enough of everything

liner large passenger ship

maiden voyage ship's first voyage

maneuver difficult movement that needs skill and planning

mast wooden or metal pole on a ship

merchant person who makes money by buying and selling goods

postponed moved to a later date

priority allowed to go first

promenade area designed for people to walk in

propeller type of fan with large blades that drives a ship forward through water

ring toss game in which players try to throw rings over spikes

rivet short type of nail that is used to hold pieces of metal together

salvage rescue something after a disaster

shipyard place where ships are built and repaired

slipway sloping area in a shipyard that leads from the land into the water

stern back end of a ship

submersible small, watertight vessel designed to operate under water

tender boat used to ferry people or supplies to and from a ship

tug boat small boat used to pull or push a larger ship through areas in which it would be difficult for the large ship to maneuver

Turkish bath hot room full of steam

FINDING OUT MORE

BOOKS

Adams, Simon. *Titanic.* New York: Dorling Kindersley, 1999.

Ballard, Robert, and Michael Sweeney. *Return to Titanic.* Washington, D.C.: National Geographic, 2004.

Crew, Gary. *Pig on the Titanic: A True Story*. New York: HarperCollins, 2005.

Fahey, Kathleen. *Titanic*. Milwaukee: Gareth Stevens, 2005.

Matsen, Bradford. *The Incredible Quest to Find the Titanic.* Berkeley Heights, N.J.: Enslow, 2003.

Molony, Senan. *Titanic: A Primary Source History*. Milwaukee: Gareth Stevens, 2005.

Morris, Mark. *Transportation.* Chicago: Heinemann Library, 2006.

WEBSITES

www.titanic-titanic.com
One of the most extensive websites about the disaster.

www.encyclopedia-titanica.org/index.php
Read detailed biographies of the passengers and crew.

www.nationalgeographic.com/ngkids/9607/titanic.html
The true story of the twelve-year-old daughter of a missionary who survived the sinking of the *Titanic*.

www.titanic-online.com
The website of RMS Titanic Inc., which is a company that recovers, conserves, and exhibits items from the *Titanic*'s wreck.

www.pbs.org/wgbh/nova/titanic
Learn about the *Britannic*, which sank during World War I off the coast of Greece. Read an interview with the explorer who found the wreck.

FURTHER RESEARCH

If you are interested in finding out more about the *Titanic*, try researching the following topics:

- The discovery of the wreck of the *Titanic*, and what is still being found under the sea.

- The great inventions in transportation that allowed people to cross the Atlantic more easily.

- The *Titanic*'s sister ship, the *Britannic* (the name eventually given to the *Gigantic*).

- Learn about the safety features of big ships.

INDEX